More and more pre-teen *girls* are going through life battling issues that they sometimes believe no one can truly understand. Thankfully, there is now a book written not just for pre-teens and teenagers, but for people from all walks of life, regardless of their age, gender, religion or race.

This book brings to life the many hidden issues pre-teens and teenagers struggle with every day. In reading this book you will find out how one young girl was able to ride the waves and weather the storms of her teenage years and with prayer, family, and friends overcome it all.

Her story, told from the heart, takes you into the depth of her struggles with cutting, anxiety, depression, anorexia, and suicide.

Shannon bared it all and through her story hopes to help other young girls and boys overcome these struggles. The details are visual and with the turn of each page you are left wanting to read more on how she broke the chains and became free from cutting, anxiety, depression, anorexia, and suicide.

—*Sherika Dacres*
Middle School Teacher

This extraordinary young woman has generously shared her personal struggle through pain, despair, and self-destructive experiences in adolescence to the other side of enthusiastically embracing life in young adulthood. To read this book is to travel with her and to believe that there is hope for others. I look forward to a sequel.

—*Margaret A. Foley, LCSW*
Social Worker

CHAINS BE
BROKEN

CHAINS BE
BROKEN

FINDING FREEDOM FROM CUTTING, ANXIETY, DEPRESSION, ANOREXIA, AND SUICIDE

SHANNON LEIGH ROWELL

Oviedo, Florida

Chains Be Broken: Finding Freedom from Cutting, Anxiety, Depression, Anorexia, and Suicide
by Shannon Leigh Rowell

Published by HigherLife Development Services, Inc.
400 Fontana Circle
Building 1 – Suite 105
Oviedo, Florida 32765
(407) 563-4806
www.ahigherlife.com

Disclaimer: While each of the stories shared is based on truthful circumstances, they have been updated to protect all parties involved.

Unless otherwise noted, Scripture quotations are from *The Holy Bible: NEW INTERNATIONAL VERSION*®. Copyright © 1973, 1978, 1984 by Biblica, Inc. All rights reserved worldwide. Used by permission.

Scripture quotations noted KJV are from *The Holy Bible: King James Version*. Public domain.

Scripture quotations noted NKJV are from the *New King James Version*. Copyright © 1982 Thomas Nelson Inc. Used by permission. All rights reserved.

ISBN 10: 1-935245-22-8

Cover Design: Judith McKittrick Wright

First Edition

10 11 12 13 — 9 8 7 6 5 4 3 2 1

Printed in the United States of America

Dedication

TO MY MOM AND DAD: I dedicate this book to my wonderful parents, Marshall and Sherrie Sitarik. I thank both of you for your continued support and encouragement in my life. You have both believed in me when no one else was willing. Although I have put you through more than any parent should have to experience with their child, I thank you from the bottom of my heart for choosing to never give up on me. I have learned a tremendous amount from my experiences and hope to make you proud by using my story to help others. Thank you for guiding me and staying with me each step of the way. I love you!

TO MY HUSBAND: I now understand if I hadn't taken the path God gave me I would not have been led to the love of my life, Steven Rowell. You are truly an amazing blessing and a wonderful man. I thank you for your unconditional love and support. I couldn't have achieved my many dreams without your encouragement. You are my stronghold, and I thank God for you each and every day. Thank you for loving me the way you do. I love you!

SPECIAL THANKS: I would like to offer a special thanks to my sister, Stacey Lynn Sitarik. I know it wasn't always easy for you to experience the trauma I was living. I feel I have put you through a tremendous amount of stress at such a young age, but no matter the cost, you have always been by my side. I want to thank you for being such a wonderful sister and best friend.

I would also like to recognize my grandmother, Beatrix Sitarik. You have always held a special place in my heart. Thank you for being my anchor when I needed you the most. I couldn't have gotten through this hard time without your love and support.

Table of Contents

Poems

All poems by Shannon Rowell

Illustrations

All illustrations by Shannon Rowell

Prologue

I AM SITTING HERE STARING out in the distance… There is a young girl; she looks as if she hasn't got a friend in the world to talk with. I can't help but wonder what she is thinking or why she looks so lonely. Surely she is normal, just like anyone else her age. There is no way she could have ever gone through or experienced what I have been through. So why does she look so sad? Why does she frown when everyone around her smiles?

Then she looks in my direction. Our eyes lock, and it is then I realize the girl I am watching is…me.

Perhaps you feel as I did. One minute you are scared and insecure, and the next, secure. You laugh and cry with the greatest of force in your life. You feel alone and scared and confused. Suddenly, change is the enemy, and you cling to the past with dear life. Soon you realize the past is wandering farther and farther away, and there is nothing to do but stay where you are or move forward. This is when you are faced with making your next life decision.

Which will you choose?

"COMMIT TO THE LORD WHATEVER YOU DO AND YOUR PLANS WILL SUCCEED."

—Proverbs 16:3

My Personal Mission Statement

First and foremost, I will remain faithful always to my God.

I will not underestimate the power of prayer.

I will not neglect true friends, but will also make time for myself.

I will respect my family and their choices.

I will live with my own consequences.

I will cross my bridges as I come to them.

I will always remain positive and be the best at everything I do.

All my intentions begin with self-revelation.

Introduction

THIS BOOK IS NOT for the faint of heart. I have pondered quite often if I would even want to write my story for others to read. I realized not everyone wants to have a conversation about their personal life experiences or let a complete stranger know their deep inner feelings. I do know, however, that many young people are going through experiences very similar to what I have had. They are afraid for whatever reason to tell someone or ask for help. As much as I would like my story to help everyone, I know this is unrealistic. I have intended this book not only to help teens and young adults who have a similar background as mine but also to help parents understand what their child or someone close to them is experiencing.

If you start to read this and are unable to relate or are just not interested, then this book may not be meant for you. However, if you start to read and find yourself longing for more understanding, then I encourage you to keep reading. My goal is to share with you a story many people would deem too personal to share with others. I am opening my heart to you now because I know without a doubt that everything happens for a reason, and there is always hope in this forever chaotic world.

Chapter 1

A Young Girl Searching

IF YOU WERE TO look at my life from the beginning, you would see what would appear to be an almost perfect life. I have a mother and father who have never been divorced, a younger sister, and have always had a dog growing up. My grandma has always had a great presence in my life and even lived with my family as I grew up. I have attended the most prestigious private Christian schools and have always lived what I would call a comfortable life.

My parents would tell you I was the perfect little girl. I used to ask permission just to get out of bed in the morning. However, once I started to hit my teenage years, my life took a major turn. In fact, even now it is hard for me to remember some of what I experienced. To help me cope I have blocked a lot of hurtful and awful memories, but there are still some memories I just can't get rid of no matter how hard I try.

A majority of it started when I was thirteen years old. I attended a very small private Christian middle school in Orlando, Florida. My parents wanted me to attend a Christian school to help reinforce the beliefs of our family.

At the time we attended church and would go to service every Sunday morning.

As I got older, I decided I wanted to attend a youth group at another church. My parents eventually agreed, and so on Wednesday nights they would drop me off for youth group where I would meet some of my friends. The second week of attending youth group I met a guy named Timothy who was a little older than I was. I was immediately attracted to the vibe he gave off. He dressed and talked differently than the people I usually hung out with. He would wear black baggy pants and usually a black Korn shirt. (Korn was a popular rock band at the time.) He was more confident than other guys and had a punkish style about him. His hair was a very dark chocolate color, almost black, and curly. We became friends almost immediately, and instead of attending youth group on Wednesday nights, a group of us would meet and walk to the nearby McDonald's to hang out until it was time for youth group to be over. After several weeks, Timothy introduced our group to another so-called religion, Wicca. I was enthralled by the darkness of this Wicca experience and tried to learn as much as I could under Timothy's guidance. He gave me a couple of books to take home to study and said when I saw him the next week he would explain anything I didn't understand.

Back at school I introduced my two closest friends to Wicca, and in after-school care we would practice the different rituals we read about. Since the school was so small, we would usually block off the girls' bathroom, turn off the lights, and dive into the different rituals explained in the book. At first it all seemed harmless and fun. The girls' bathroom had a long countertop, and one of us usually lay on the counter while the other two girls summoned spirits around her. I think we would even spook ourselves and just think things were happening around us that really weren't.

It was, however, witchcraft. I soon became so involved in witchcraft that I would study and practice it under my parents' roof. I knew I started to get into the heavy stuff when the nightmares started. Almost every night I would have a recurring nightmare of four dark hooded figures appearing out of my closets. They would stand over me as I was sleeping and whisper to me. They would tell me to kill myself or hurt others to help release the pain I was feeling. Each night the nightmares went further and further and became more vivid. Although I was sleeping, it felt so real. I could feel the cold energy as they placed their hands slightly above my body. I could hear the whispers as they spoke to me, getting louder each time they appeared. There were nights when I would try to tell myself to wake up, but I just couldn't. When I would finally awake, I would be drenched in sweat and often wonder if it truly was a just a dream.

Whispers
November 15, 1999

Voices in my head tell me,
They whisper evil thoughts
To make me believe.
They say it won't hurt.
It will happen so fast;
That I won't feel a thing,
And the day will finally be my last.
I guess I'm starting to believe
There's tons of ways to do it,
As long as I make myself bleed.
I'm really starting to think,
Should I use this knife?
Take these pills lying here?
Or just find another way to take my life?
You ask why should I do it.
Well, if you knew what I've been going
    through
You'd probably be debating it too.
OK, I'm standing on the edge.
I take the knife; stab it in my chest,
And finally fall off the ledge.
That's it, I did it!
The voices are gone,
My family's upset,
And now I don't have to go on.

With each passing day I would fall deeper into a depressed state. I felt I was literally falling in a dark hole with no way out. It was a horrible feeling because I didn't know or even understand why I felt so empty inside. I quickly became anorexic and slept all the time, and when I was awake I was so miserable others didn't want to be around me. I started to think of ways to make the inner pain stop, and then I remembered what the hooded figures in my nightmares told me to do. I started to think of ways to kill myself, but I wasn't even sure it was something I could really do. For the next couple of months, I wrote a lot. I started writing poetry to get what I was feeling out and onto paper, but it wasn't enough. Every moment I had, I would sleep. As long as I was sleeping I didn't feel the pain. I didn't have to constantly feel like a knife was penetrating my heart, and I didn't have to be around anyone. I just couldn't take it anymore. I didn't even know why I felt so much pain in my life.

One night I was lying with my mom in her bedroom, as I usually did to spend time with her, and I mustered up the courage to tell her I didn't want to live anymore. As you can imagine, this took her by surprise. She immediately started to ask me questions and soon realized I was experiencing something very deep and painful that would require professional help.

Suicidal Note

May 17, 1999

I say good-bye to my friends and family
And to all the people who have hurt me.
I say good-bye to my dog
So that I might go to heaven and be with
    God.
I'm sorry I have to tell you this way,
But there's really not much more I can say.
I'm tired of my life so I have to go,
But remember, Mom, how much I love you
    so.
I can't live in misery anymore,
For my heart's already been torn.
And I want you to remember it's not your
    fault.
I chose to do this
To get away from it all.
Remember I love you
But now I must say good-bye.
You are the best parents
So please don't cry.

Please note that I did not intend to give this note to
my parents. Writing poetry was an outlet for me, and
although I was contemplating suicide, I chose to express
my feelings on paper rather than through actions.

Chapter 2

Funny Farm

THE DAY AFTER I told my mom my thoughts, I went to school like normal—except the day turned out to be far from any other normal day. Then again, I don't think I even knew what normal was anymore. Right after class was dismissed for lunch, I saw my mom and her best friend coming down the hallway. I was surprised to see them, and when I approached them, my mom was barely able to speak to me. Her best friend took me in her arms and told me that I needed to come with them. I soon learned I would be going to a psychiatric treatment facility because I was having "suicidal ideations," which is just fancy talk for having thoughts about killing myself.

I cried all the way home. I was told to go to my room and pack a couple of different outfits because they didn't know how long I would be in the hospital. As soon as I got to my room, I quickly picked up the phone and dialed my then-boyfriend Nick and told him what was going on. I can't remember the extent of our conversation, but I remember him being supportive and trying to calm me down.

Imagine being a thirteen-year-old girl and being told you are going to be hospitalized for having thoughts to hurt yourself. I was terrified! Why were my parents doing this to me, and what would they decide to do if they knew even half of what I was into? So I kept the nightmares and Wicca a secret just a little bit longer.

When we got to the hospital, my mom and her friend registered me. I was so mad at my mom that I didn't even say good-bye to her. My heart was pounding and tears flowed down my cheeks. I was hot, literally. My hands were sweating and I felt like I couldn't breathe. I wasn't crazy! I didn't belong in a place like this. What if the others in the center hurt me?

I gave my mom's friend a hug and walked down a long hallway with a nurse. I remember being terrified and mad at the same time. My mother worked at the same organization as this hospital, so they told me I had to register under an alias. I chose my best friend's last name and was given an armband. The only perk to my mother's job position was getting my own room. Usually patients have to share a room that has a pair of twin beds, a dresser, and one bathroom. The walls were bright white and the floor was utterly cold. I can remember the empty feeling of sitting in my room. It was very depressing.

As I entered my room, the nurse told me she would need to do a skin check on me. *What the hell is that?* I wondered. *You want to do what? Are you crazy?* She told me to undress so that I could show her any marks on my body. I was humiliated! It was so cold, and I cried the entire time. I felt I was being stripped of my dignity.

If you are a parent reading this, you can probably empathize with my mom when she had to make this difficult decision to admit me to the hospital. As angry as I was with her, I know she made this decision based on what she thought was best for me at the time. Just as any mother would do, this was the only way she felt I would be protected. I needed intense treatment and had to get out of the toxic environment I was in.

BASKET CASE

Basket Case

It took a couple days before the doctor would even see me. Each day would be the same, almost like the movie *Groundhog Day* when the same thing happened day after day—except for me it was in a more confined area. A typical day for me in the psychiatric center consisted of waking up early, having my vital signs taken, eating breakfast, cleaning my room, watching the morning news, group therapy, school, and some free time. Because I was anorexic I had to be watched closely when it came to meal time. I can remember trying to hide my food or give it away when no one was looking. Why should they be able to choose whether I ate or not? When it came time for me to have my vitals taken and be weighed, the staff would make me turn backward on the scale so I couldn't see how much I weighed. Every time I stepped foot on the scale I felt I was growing bigger and bigger, and it only made me want to eat less to stop the thoughts of feeling fat.

Feeling Good
September 29, 1999

My body is feeling tired and alone
But yet I strive to be the smallest,
The only kind of my own.
When I look in the mirror all I see is fat.
People say I'm nothing but skin and bones
But it feels like I'm much more than that.
I starve myself thinking I'll be OK,
But when I listen to others,
"You're going to die" is all they say.
I want to feel good about myself

And if that means not eating
Then I'll do that to risk my health.
Sooner or later I know I'll die,
But at least I felt good about myself
When I was still alive.

Free time consisted of watching television, reading, or developing my poetic skills. We would have to earn points to use the telephone, and it was required that one of our calls be made to our parents. I would always somehow get around calling my mom and dad and would call Nick instead. He seemed to be the only person not against me at the time.

I was in the center for over two weeks and even had to spend my fourteenth birthday there. Do you think I got a cake or even gifts? No! When it came time for visitation, I was always excited to see my grandma. I missed her more than anyone. She would always write me letters, and after our visit I would open and read them. Looking back I can see how I was breaking her heart. My parents and I started to drift farther and farther away, and I wasn't able to see my sister because she was a minor and the hospital wouldn't allow minors to visit. As much as we didn't get along at the time, there was always a part of me that longed for her to be near.

After a couple of days, I started to open up to some of the staff and other patients. I started to learn the right comments I should give in order to make it seem as if

I were getting better. There was one tech in particular I remember the most. He would read the poems I wrote and encourage me to keep writing to express myself. That made such an impact on me that I wrote a poem dedicated to him while I was in the center.

Closed Doors
March 25, 1999

Sitting quiet and still
In the darkest room;
I'm tired of begging and being here
Behind closed doors.
Nothing ever seems to work.
I'm very uncomfortable
And just want to leave this earth.
I don't need help;
Just want to be left alone
So I can be by myself.

I met one girl while I was hospitalized who was a few years older than I. We became good friends during my stay. As we exchanged stories, she told me of another way I could release the pain I was feeling without anyone noticing. That is how I learned to become a cutter. She told me she would cut herself with a blade or knife, and it helped her release her anger and pain. Of course I was up for anything at that point. I wanted to die, so this couldn't hurt. The only problem was being stuck in the psychiatric hospital where there were no sharp objects.

One day I asked to get a picture out of my wallet, and when the nurse handed it to me I realized I had left a Coke bottle cap in the front fold. I took it out with the picture so the nurse wouldn't notice. I quickly went back to my room and started to act as if I were reading a magazine. I learned the schedule of the timed checkups that the techs had to perform and knew I had exactly fifteen minutes to try to cut myself until they would be back to check on me. I bit the cap in half and put it to my arm. I pushed down as hard as I could and dragged it across my arm until I saw the blood. After the initial slit it became so easy.

I remember it feeling so good to see and feel the blood starting to drip down my arm. I was able to carve the word *vampire* on my left arm that day—except I spelled the word wrong: VAMPIER. To keep from getting noticed I wore long sleeves and baggy sweatshirts all the time. No one suspected a thing because it was always cold in the hospital, and so I went unnoticed for the rest of my stay. This was the day I became addicted to cutting, which would be a lifelong battle. It felt great to finally control when I felt pain and to have the scars as a constant reminder of the pain I had inside.

Looking back I can't believe how young I was when I started to feel and act the way I did. It's hard to believe that anyone would take a blade or any sharp object to their flesh and actually enjoy it. I'm sure people wonder how anyone could take the pain of cutting themselves, but truthfully I didn't feel any pain as I did it. I actually felt relieved. I could feel the pressure and flesh splitting. The blood smelled of iron and was warm as it dripped down my arm. I would let the wounds almost heal and then pick the scabs off to make it bleed again. Sometimes I would cut to punish myself for thoughts or feelings I had.

After two weeks of my hospitalization and trying to fool the staff into thinking I was getting better, I received word that the doctors finally felt I was on the road to recovery and was ready to go home. I remember being terrified after leaving the hospital because I was now on my own. I didn't feel safe anymore and I didn't want to tell anyone I was scared because I didn't want to show any signs of weakness.

My first night home I had my best friend spend the night with me. I decided to show her my arm and told her how I learned to cut myself. I asked her not to tell anyone and promised it was only cutting to release the pain and not an attempt to kill myself. While she promised she would keep it a secret, my mom later found out when she walked in on me taking a bath. She was shocked and ran out of my room sobbing. At that moment I started to feel bad, a feeling I rarely felt toward others.

I got dressed and went to talk to my mom. I found her in our backyard sitting in a chair crying. I went up to her and gave her a hug. I told her that I was really in need of help because I didn't care if I died that day or any day soon. I didn't see a point to my life. My mom held me and told me she would never give up on me. She slept with me for many nights and almost never left my side. Whenever she had the chance, she would rub vitamin E oil on my scars to help them fade.

Fallen Soul
June 2, 2000

I wonder if there's a hole in my soul.
My life doesn't feel complete
And I feel I've fallen
In a complete and utterly dark hole.
The pain cuts within.
The hole gets deeper,
The cutting begins.

I was put into counseling right away. I saw a psychiatrist who prescribed for me antidepressants. I was put on the highest dose, which later would take me a year to wean off when I was feeling better. I began counseling with a pastor at a local church. After just one session, this Christian counselor told my mom to give up on me and that there was nothing that anyone could ever do to help me. In fact, he told my mother there is a very low recovery rate for kids involved with cults. I was a lost cause. My mom was devastated but refused to believe him. I never did go back to that counselor. In fact, his own son later experienced some of the same things I was battling. Sadly this boy took his own life. I'm not sure if this counselor decided to follow the same advice he had given my mother.

My mother wouldn't give up. Instead I kept seeing my psychiatrist and later saw another counselor whom I liked a lot. For a while I started to get better. I stopped practicing Wicca and started to feel less pain. My poetry turned from dark and depressing to writing more about love. I still felt depressed a lot, and at times it took me awhile to convince myself to get out of bed, but I did graduate from middle school and convinced my parents it was time for me to stop attending private Christian schools. So off I went to my first public high school.

Chapter 3

A Taste of the Real World

I ENTERED HIGH SCHOOL IN ninth grade, and it wasn't long before I met quite a few different people. Immediately I became friends with the Goths. I started to wear all black clothes, heavy black makeup, and even had my hair partially red at times. I started to identify myself with them.

They Called Him a Freak
November 7, 1998

Dressed in black
From head to toe;
Walking the streets
But staying low.
Never a word did he speak,
But it was with his looks
That made the people freak.
From his dead black hair,
To the dark makeup that he wore
Is what made the people's hearts tear.
And never once did anyone come near

To lend him a simple hand;
But instead they watched in fear.
Because of the carvings on his arms
It gave him a look
Without a charm.
He was just like any other guy
But now he was all alone
Because no one gave it a try
To understand the question, why?
So they called him a FREAK!

I met a guy named Damien in one of my classes. Like many other guys I met, he was much older than I was. Are you starting to see a recurring theme yet? We began to date, and during this time I was introduced to drugs. I started to smoke a lot of marijuana, or weed. In fact, I got high before I ever even tried smoking a cigarette.

My first encounter with weed was a complete adrenaline rush. Damien and I were in the car with a couple of our friends from school driving down the back roads of our town. We pulled over on a dirt road and lit a joint. Next thing I knew they "hot boxed" the car, which means they sealed all the windows and doors so that smoke filled the car. I didn't feel anything until we finally opened the car door to let the smoke out. As I stepped out of the car I was so dizzy I could barely stand, but it was a freeing feeling, and I had only inhaled the secondhand smoke. After that day I started to smoke whenever I could get my hands on it. When I was high I would do things I never thought of doing before, and I liked the risk. I became more outspoken and adventurous. I thought I was invincible.

I was living life free and loved every minute of it—yet I became more and more depressed, suicidal, anorexic, and addicted to cutting. My thinking soon became so distorted that at times I would try any drug or do anything harmful to myself because I thought it would take me one step closer to dying. Sometimes I didn't even know what I was taking. I remember taking a drug once, and within minutes I started to feel foggy, dizzy, and disoriented. I was watching TV and instead of seeing people I was seeing their skeletons. I started to become freaked out, but it soon faded and then became enjoyable. I also liked the feeling because I was able to tune my family out and not care about what they had to say or what they were feeling. In addition to cutting, I started to pierce different body parts on my own. I loved the feeling of a needle penetrating my skin. I would later have to take the piercing out due to infection.

2 Beer Queer

September 2, 2003

My mind goes blank
On the most clearest of days;
My brain has been shot,

Frozen over in a haze.
My speech is slurred
And my lips are numb;
The limbs of my body
To slush they have become.
My stomach turns
And I begin to feel faint;
My feet give underneath me
But never yet a complaint.
My vision is blurred;
I can no longer see;
Everything becomes cold
And I no longer believe.
I'm starting to feel good,
Yet tired it seems;
I passed out on my bed
No longer to be seen.

During this period of my life I developed many unhealthy relationships. One night I was hanging out with one of my friends at the golf course where he worked. I remember talking to him as he was cleaning up the store. It was late and we were the only ones around. I followed him out to the course to help him clean up the golf balls that were on the ground. Next thing I knew he had me pinned down on the ground and was taking off my pants. I can remember telling him "No!" several times, but he raped me. For some reason I wasn't strong enough, physically or mentally, to struggle.

I went home and acted like nothing ever happened. I started to think I brought it on myself and that maybe it wasn't really considered rape because I didn't fight enough to make him stop. I did not tell anyone for several years. In fact, I still hung out with this guy on several other occasions. It wasn't until much later that I realized what had really taken place that night. When my counselors would suspect I was sexually abused, I would deny it full force. I didn't want to believe it happened, and I didn't want anyone to know. It wasn't until seven years later that I actually told my mom. And my suspicions were right about how she would react. She started to cry and was so upset that I felt horrible!

I was only fifteen years old, and I had just experienced what no one should ever have to experience. I thought he was one of my friends. Why would a friend do something like that to someone? Did I truly deserve it? I remember it being very dark outside. It happened behind a bush. Funny thing is I have been back to that golf course since then and the bush is no longer there. Why did this make me second guess what happened? It felt so real. I was cold. I could feel the prickles of the grass that for some reason made me itch. I could feel the pressure of his hands holding me down with his weight. I gave up and stopped fighting.

The recurring nightmares that I had previously returned fairly soon after that night. This time, however, I had not only had thoughts of killing myself but also thoughts to hurt others in my family. One night I woke up from a nightmare and started to scream. When my mom came into my room she said I looked straight at her and started to curse. I don't remember what I said, but unfortunately I do remember yelling. Although I wanted to stop, for some reason I couldn't. A couple of minutes later I snapped out of it and seemed myself again.

Although we weren't sure what that night was about, my mom prayed over my room and my closets, because this was where I used to practice the witchcraft. In fact, in one of my walk-in closets, which was more like a storage room, the light would turn on frequently in the middle of the night all by itself for no reason. Eventually my parents put a deadbolt lock on that door. The light continued to flick on randomly and only stopped a couple of years ago.

The dreams and pain I was experiencing became so intense that I would literally hug the floor of my bedroom every night and cry. I would cry and cry and constantly ask God why He was keeping me alive. I would beg and plead for Him to let it all end. When nothing would happen, I would get so angry that I would start to cut myself again until the blood ran down my flesh.

Unborn

August 24, 2000

Lord, are You there?
I call Your name,
But do You care?
Do You know the struggles,
Trials and labors
That are within me?
I've surely prayed,
But now all I
Do is pay.
Guide me, Jesus,
Set me free!
Keep Your promise
So I'll believe.

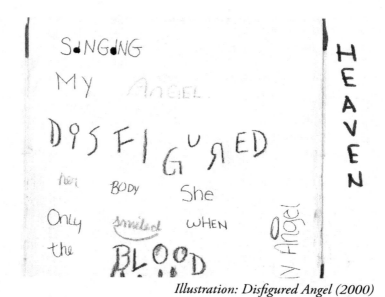

Illustration: Disfigured Angel (2000)

My relationship with my father continued to grow even more distant. For some reason I would take everything out on him because I didn't trust him. I hated to be left alone in our house with him when my mom would have to work late nights. Although my dad never did or would ever intentionally hurt me, I was scared. I thought he might hurt me just as I was hurt on the golf course. I felt I had no control over anything, except my weight— no control over my life or the direction it was heading. I didn't trust anyone anymore. When I would fall asleep at night, I would immediately wake up if anyone even came near my room. I could sense the slightest presence of anyone near me as I slept and would open my eyes to see who and why they were coming near me so late at night.

Chapter 4

Valentine Nightmare

I WOULD LOOK FORWARD TO going to high school every day because I was able to have more freedom and spend time with my friends. I would skip class and hang out with Damien and a couple of others smoking weed in the bathrooms. On February 14, 1999, Damien was expelled from school for dealing drugs, and I decided I would skip school to go hang out with him at his place for the day. I got a ride from one of the guys in an older grade and was dropped off at Damien's house, just down the street from where my parents lived. Instead of trying to remember and summarize what happened that day, here is a story I wrote on that actual day:

"Yes," Shannon agreed, as she started to pass on her way up to her room. She was only fifteen years old and yet she felt she already knew the meaning of the word *love*. Shannon was a bright young lady even though she knew she had made many mistakes in the past. Everything started when Shannon met Damien, a guy at school. She knew as soon as she saw him that she would connect on a whole different level with him. Her parents on the other hand despised Damien and forbid her to see him— but of course, Shannon had her own plans as she always did.

When Shannon reached her room, she immediately picked up the phone and started to dial. She was very careful of the words she chose as she told Damien the conversation she had just had with her parents about not seeing him anymore. Damien told her that nothing could ever stand in the way of his love for her, which made Shannon feel even more important.

For the next couple of months she kept her relationship with Damien a secret. She continued to see him by lying to her parents. She would hide their relationship by telling her parents that she was going to a friend's house down the street. Damien would even sneak into her house when her parents had left or weren't paying attention.

During this time, Shannon began to grow even further away from her parents and friends. Eventually Damien was expelled from school and got a full-time job, and they were seldom able to see each other.

On February 14, 1999, Shannon skipped school and got a ride to Damien's home. She never thought she would get caught, but little did she know what was about to happen. At the end of the day, Shannon called her dad, and while pretending to be at school she asked if she could stay late. Her dad knew by this time that Shannon was lying and told her to meet him up at the school in ten minutes. On the way to the school Shannon told Damien everything that was said on the phone with her dad. Damien told her that if her dad hurt her in any way that he was just a phone call away.

As Shannon got out of the car, she kissed Damien good-bye and began proceeding up the long flight of stairs. As she reached her father, he grabbed her by the arm and made her get into his car. He told her that he knew everything and he wanted her to show him where Damien lived. After driving to the wrong house a couple of times, Shannon took him to Damien's house.

As they approached the house, Shannon ran out of the car and began to bang on Damien's front door. Once Damien let her in, she quickly ran and hid behind him. Shannon's father yelled at both of them. He asked Damien if he had sex with his daughter, and while Shannon was shaking her head no, Damien told him yes. Shannon's father was furious. Once he finished yelling at Damien, he took Shannon and dragged her out the door. The yelling didn't stop until he finally got Shannon in the car. As soon as she was in the car, Shannon motioned for Damien to call the cops.

As soon as they got home, Shannon's father went into her room and started to throw things out the second-story window. Electronics were flying and hitting the pavement. It was all too much for Shannon to take. She ran to the kitchen and took a handful of aspirin. Based on previous attempts, she knew she hadn't taken nearly enough to kill herself, but her father wouldn't know the difference. To make her father stop, she yelled to him what she had just done and told him there was nothing he could do about it and that it was too late. This got her father to stop throwing her things out the window.

In anger, her father dialed 911. He told them what had happened and within moments the ambulance was at the house. They took Shannon's vitals and spoke to her without her father present. When everything seemed to be OK, Shannon proceeded to tell them that her father was abusive. She showed them the bruise on her ankle, which was made by the car door slamming on it, but the cops didn't need

to know that part. In the meantime, Shannon's
father called her mother and gave her a head's
up on what was going on. She immediately
rushed home.

I wrote that as a story, but it is exactly what happened
on that day. The police told my parents they would
need to take me to a psychiatric facility, but my parents
refused because that was where I had learned to cut in my
previous admission. So the police made my parents sign
a waiver saying they were refusing to send me with them
for treatment.

My parents also had to sign a waiver for my psycholo-
gist stating they were responsible for my life. My parents
felt I was better off at home with them since I had learned
unhealthy ways of coping in my previous admittance to
the hospital.

Once the police left, my father came into my room and
told me that what he was doing was not considered a form
of abuse. He was so hurt by the accusations of abuse that
he left the house. After a while, things started to settle
down, but my life would be again forever changed. What
a horrible feeling my dad must have felt when his oldest
daughter accused him of such a horrible act and in public.
How could I have done something so awful to a father
who was forgiving and supportive?

After that my parents began to think about sending me
to a home for troubled teens. They had the papers on the

counter, and all they had to do was sign on the line. I still don't know why they never sent me, but I was pulled out of the public high school and was homeschooled for half a year by my dad. My dad would wake me up every day at 8:00 a.m. and make me sit downstairs near his office to do school work. I hated every minute of it. I remember crying almost every day, especially when I would see my friends walking home after school. I felt so confined and trapped. My parents had taken the hinges off my bedroom door and put a tap on our house phone line. I had no privacy and was not allowed to be left alone very often.

My mom has since told me that she and my father went to a spy shop to buy a caller ID system to monitor my incoming and outgoing calls. They said it was one of the strangest stores they had ever stepped foot in, and they felt very out of place. I found many ways to get around this monitoring. When I wanted to talk to someone my parents did not allow me to talk to, I would call a friend and have them three-way call that person so that my friend's number would show up instead of the main person I wanted to talk to. My friend would usually set the phone down and let me talk to the other person on the three-way call, and we would hang up when we were done. I would also have my friends buy pre-paid phone cards to call me. This way the phone could not be traced by my parents.

CADS
(Cutting, Anxiety, Depression, Suicide)
January 21, 2004

Distorted in the mind,
Fogged by a cloud,
Something that can't be defined.
Thoughts that make no sense,
With visions and words
That will make one become tense.
Breathing only gets harder,
Anxiety attacks
With chest pains only getting tighter.
The room starts spinning;
The pain deepens within;
The question to be asked...
"When will this end?"
Cutting, it becomes a source;
Seeing the blood
Only releases the hurt.
And now the end to the beginning,
Contemplating suicide
Only to attempt it beyond one's mind.
All four in one together;
Cutting, Anxiety, Depression, & Suicide,
Forever becoming a solution to life.

Without my knowledge, my parents started to do routine checks in my room and go through my bags, trash, mattress, and drawers. My mom would take notes I had written back and forth with my friends and keep track of who was and wasn't a good influence on me.

One day my dad found a pack of cigarettes in my purse and started yelling at me, saying he couldn't believe I was smoking and that I didn't know what I was doing to myself. I remember thinking how crazy he was because cigarettes should have been the least of his worries. I had started to smoke only when I wasn't able to get my hands on other drugs.

My parents took away my music. I was listening to a tremendous amount of songs about suicide, which reinforced my thoughts to hurt myself. I felt the words of the songs I was listening to were the only words that related to how I felt. The more songs I would listen to, the more engulfed in darkness I became.

I had just gotten my driver's permit and loved to drive, but I couldn't drive without an adult in the car, so my mom realized that driving with me was a good opportunity for her to talk to me. I couldn't exactly go anywhere inside the car. At the same time, my parents knew I needed a professional to talk with, so they put me into counseling. I rarely wanted to open up to my parents, but somehow it seemed easier to talk to someone outside my family.

I started to go back to the other church for youth group on Wednesday nights just to be able to get out of the house. My parents would sit outside the church building every Wednesday to make sure I didn't leave until it was over.

I soon realized the only way I would be able to see Damien and the rest of my friends my parents didn't approve of was to invite them to church. So I would continue to see Damien at church, and on occasions when my parents weren't sitting outside the doors to the church, we would skip the service and go across the street to Popeye's to hang out. Church soon became my outlet from the prison I was living in at home, and all seemed well to my parents because I wasn't fighting them anymore and was attending church. Little did they know I was continuing to rebel.

One day I asked my parents if one of my friends could come over and spend the night. With good intentions, my parents agreed. They were happy I was finally making some friends and was allowing them to meet the friends. So I brought my friend Tracey home to meet my parents. When Tracey arrived, we walked out to the back porch to say hello to my parents. Tracey was dressed in black from head to toe and had many body piercings. She had jet black hair and wore heavy black makeup. I can only imagine what my parents were thinking as she walked up to them and started to talk.

I remember my dad looking straight at her. "Let me ask you a question," he said. "You're not, like, going to kill us in the middle of the night, are you?" I was mortified! Looking back now, it was kind-of humorous. Tracey was actually a very nice person, but needless to say my parents slept with their door locked that night.

After my parents homeschooled me for my freshman year of high school, they decided to put me back into a private Christian school. I hated that idea! There was a new private Christian school down the road from my house. My parents took me to meet the dean of the school, and he gave us an application packet to fill out. I hated the idea of being put back into a private school, so I refused to complete the application forms. My parents had to fill them out for me and even had to make up my mission statement. The school required each applicant to tell the story of how he or she came to be a Christian, and because I wasn't a Christian yet, my parents had to fill it out for me. Needless to say I got accepted into the school and began my sophomore year in 2001.

Because it was a private school I could no longer wear all black. I was required to wear a uniform every day and adhere to very strict rules. I absolutely hated it! I felt I could only be myself on the weekends, when I was free to dress and act as I liked. I didn't make very many friends right away, and I really didn't want to. I would get dropped off for school in the morning, and when I got home I would immediately go to my room and fall asleep.

During this time, I was also being weaned off my anti-depressant medication and started to have bad withdrawal symptoms. I was always tired and had horrible headaches. I started to turn to other avenues to help with the physical pain. That's when I started popping pills. I would take anything I could get my hands on, usually some form of pain medication, which helped me get through the long days. I would crave more and more painkillers as the days went on. Eventually, I was dropped to the lowest dose of my antidepressant and stayed on that for the next couple of years.

I still didn't want to eat or gain weight, so at lunch I would sit in the bathroom until it was time for class. When I got home I would usually tell my parents that I had either already eaten or had a very late and big lunch. It seemed to work most of the time, but when it didn't and I was forced to eat, I would revert to throwing it up as soon as I was finished and then making a cut on my body somewhere to remind myself of what I had done. I even started to wear a thick rubber band around my wrist with the words *no sugar* written in black permanent marker. This too helped to remind me not to eat anything that would cause me to gain weight.

I found many things would help with food cravings. I would train my mind to think I was full every time my stomach would growl and then smoke or take pills to help suppress the hunger feeling. I hated myself and the way I looked.

Illustration: All Beauty Has Become (2000)

I would have to say one of the major turning points in my life was when I joined my high school cheerleading team. Why in the world would I do that? I wanted to get out of the house as much as possible, and when I heard they were having varsity cheerleading tryouts, I decided I would give it a try. I had been a gymnast when I was younger, so I already knew how to tumble. How hard could it be? I showed up for tryouts dressed in all black with heavy black makeup and chains hanging from my waist. I was the only one trying out who knew how to tumble, so I made the squad. I cheered for the rest of high school and even some in college. My high school cheerleading coach told me years later that when I first showed up to try out she thought I was crazy and didn't want me on the squad. However, because I was one of the best she decided to give me a chance. And good thing she did because I had a lot of fun cheering and even helped our squad win a couple of national and state competitions.

Chapter 5

Turning Point

MY LIFE WAS STARTING to turn around in a more positive direction. I continued to go to church with my parents on a regular basis. One evening the pastor asked if anyone would like to get to know Jesus on a more personal level. He invited those who did to meet an usher at the front of the room. Having sat through many of these with me, my parents didn't think I would ever come to know Christ—but on this night something was different. I felt a tugging feeling and something told me it was time. I stood up from my seat and moved out into the aisle. My parents thought I was going to run away during the service, but instead I began walking toward the front of the room. After twenty minutes of talking with a nice lady, I walked out to meet my family. My mom was stunned when she saw me walking toward her. As I reached my family, I leaned in and told them I had accepted Christ into my life and asked Him to be my personal Savior and was now a Christian. My parents couldn't believe what they were hearing. I made sure they knew it was my decision and that I still had a lot I would need to work through. My

parents were so happy at that moment that they hugged
me for what seemed like forever.

Daddy
August 24, 2000

Daddy,
I see Thee in white
Sitting on Thy throne;
Angels to Thy right
And the devil below.
Daddy,
Why a happy face?
For when Thy eyes look upon me,
They should see such a disgrace.
Daddy,
Thy heart is pure
But blood drips down
For my cure.
Daddy,
Why?
Help me to see,
Why You suffered
To set me free.

Temptation Is Fearful
June 10, 2003

Help me, Lord,
I'm crying to Thee;
I've made mistakes
And was blind as can be.
I pray, forgive me
For what I have done;
Cleanse my soul
From being the awful one.
I could have helped myself,
And the path was clear;
And now because of temptation
All I have is fear.
You are the only one
That can save me now;
Cleanse my heart and soul
And to You I bow.
I need my life back;
I can't live knowing,
Because of my sin
·Everything I have is going.
You are the sovereign one,
And to You I pray,
Give me a second chance
That I may live to see another day.

I still continued to see a counselor, and although I didn't stop smoking or popping pills right away, I did gradually begin to cut down on my use. I started to date a guy named Thomas who was a year ahead of me in school, and my parents loved him. We dated for three and a half years, and I owe a tremendous amount of thanks to him. He really helped me get out of some bad habits. And what was even better was my parents trusted him, so I was able to get out of the house for longer periods of time. I told him a lot about my past, and he did everything he could to try to get me back on the right path. He wouldn't allow me to listen to rock music when I was around him because I would usually become so involved with the music that I would start becoming depressed. He always made sure we were hanging out with friends who had a positive influence and that we did activities that were safe and acceptable. I'm not going lie; I would steal a couple of his rock CDs every once in a while and listen to them, but for the most part he was a great influence on me and helped me transform into the person I am today.

I eventually stopped wearing all black all the time and quit smoking. I also stopped changing my hair color and decided to stick with blonde hair. I also started to become closer to my family and would attend our yearly family vacations again. By my senior year I had stopped cutting so much, quit smoking, quit popping pills, and began to wear other-colored clothes. I was transforming out of my dark stages and into a happier, lighter stage of my life.

Although I didn't necessarily enjoy my high school years because I was put back into a private school, these years were the transition period in my life. My family made it a point to take control of the situation and monitored me more closely. I was surrounded by positive influences everywhere I turned, such as the music and movies I was allowed to listen to and watch, the people I was allowed to hang out with, and the clothes I was allowed to wear.

Illustration: Struggle to Become My Own Person (2001)

After I graduated from high school in 2003, I decided it was time for me to leave the house. I moved to Jacksonville, Florida, with a good friend and attended college at the University of North Florida for the next four years. I started to gain a lot of my freedom back and even began to feel better about myself. I still wrote a lot of poetry, but instead of always writing about death, I would write more about daily life struggles and love. For once I was discovering who I truly was, not who I thought I should be.

Changing Paths
February 4, 2003

So many decisions come my way,
So many choices to make it this day.
My mind is fogged,
My head aches;
I think to myself,
What about mistakes?
I wonder what will happen
When I finally leave this place;
I want to think I won't be a disgrace.
Starting over is what I have to do;
Lead a different life
Than the one that hurts me through and
    through.
New friends will come my way,

And maybe I won't have to pretend
What I do now to fit in.
A couple of months and I'm on my own,
Leading my life down a different road.

I did great in college and loved being away from Orlando. I swore to myself that I would never return to what I thought of as a "God-awful" city. I finally understood the reason I went through so much pain. I pursued a degree in psychology and was able to help many other young girls who were going through something so similar to what I had been through. I knew this was my calling.

While in college I cheered for a year, gained some weight, joined a sorority, and became a part of the psychology club. Don't get me wrong, I partied a lot and skipped a lot of classes to go to the beach, but I felt a lot better about myself and my life. I graduated college in 2007 with a bachelor of science in psychology and a minor in sociology. I now hold a master's degree in mental health counseling from Nova Southeastern University. I know, I just said I hated Orlando, but now I live here once again—and this is why: I met the love of my life!

I am about to tell you about my life as it is today, so if all you wanted to read about was the hard times I experienced when I was younger, then put the book down now or turn to Chapter 7, A Voice. However, I believe it is important to share this new chapter in my life with you so that you can see how far I have come. I hope it also instills a little glimpse of hope for you and your family's future.

In a Man...
February 4, 2003

I want a man who loves me,
Someone to trust and to hold me.
I want a man who knows me,
Who is not afraid to understand
The trials of my past.
I want romance and laughter,
And a long life to look after.
I want a shoulder to cry on
When I'm in need;
I want someone to talk to, please.
I want to be comfortable
And not have to look my best;
I want him to love me through
Every test.
When I don't look my best
And it's all because of PMS,
I want to know he won't judge me,
But take me in his arms and
Forever love me.
I want to know it's going to last forever,
And I want to hear him say,
He loves me every day of the year.

Chapter 6

The Story of Our Love

STEVE WAS BORN IN Miami, Florida, on March 30, 1979. He was raised by his wonderful mother. Steve has one younger sibling, with whom he is very close. Because his father was in and out of his life, Steve quickly took on the role of the protector in his family. He started his own business when he fourteen years old and continued to grow in other fields of interests throughout the years. Now he is a general contractor and doing very well. He bought his first home at age twenty-one and lived there with his sister and the young woman who at the time was his fiancée. He had been engaged to her for a couple years but felt something was missing.

That's when I came along. You already know a lot of my story. I was born in Orlando, Florida, on March 28, 1985. I was raised by my mother and father and am very close to my grandmother. I have one younger sibling, Stacey, who just so happens to have the same first and middle name as Steve's sister. I attended private Christian schools for most of my education and graduated with a bachelor's degree from a public university—the University of North Florida—in May 2007. I also just recently graduated with my master's degree in mental health counseling from Nova Southeastern University.

I have always believed things happen for a reason and that God has chosen a mate for every person. Having said that, let me tell you the story of how Steve and I met. It all began with my dad, a group of his friends, and a ski trip. Ever since I was a young girl, my family has always enjoyed going on snow skiing vacations. My dad and a group of men even started the Orlando Ski Club. They met once a year for a week in January to go on a guys' ski trip to Utah. A week later, the women would fly out and meet the men for another week of skiing. For a couple of years, my best friend, Emily, and I would meet our dads in Utah to go skiing.

In 2006, the guys decided to do a combined ski trip with everyone going together. I was still in college and home on break, so I could go. Emily, however, was not able to go, and I was very reluctant to go by myself—but I decided to join them. My dad told me we would share a vehicle with his friend, who was my dentist, Dr. Ross, and someone named Steve, whom I assumed was the same age as my dad. The night before the trip, I was very ill. In fact I almost did not go, but something pushed me to go.

Very early the next morning, my dad and I drove to the Orlando airport. As we were standing at the gate ready to board the flight to Utah, Steve walked up to my dad and shook his hand. He was definitely not my dad's age; in fact, he was my age. Before he could even introduce himself, I immediately thought, *This is the guy I am going to marry.* As he shook my hand, I tried to stop the thought that was going through my mind and snap out of it, but I knew there was something different about him.

Somehow we both forgot the fact that we had significant others back home. My dad even kept mentioning something about Steve's wife. I went through the entire first day in Utah thinking Steve was married and there was no chance of anything ever coming about. Then later that day, Dr. Ross tried to put my dad in his place by saying Steve wasn't married, only engaged. By this time I was really confused.

The next night at dinner we had barbeque. No one seemed to be talking, so I decided to use the opportunity to get some information. I looked up at Steve, who was sitting across from me, and said "Wait a minute. You're not married and you don't have a ring on your finger. So what are you?"

As you can imagine, Steve was completely floored!

"Shannon, you're being rude!" my dad said. "Stop asking so many questions."

Dr. Ross, however, darted right in there. "Yeah, Steve. What are you two?"

Steve thought about it for a minute or two and then said, "Well, she's my girlfriend." He went on to explain that he wasn't very happy in his relationship and had a lot to think about.

The next morning Steve was very quiet when he came down for breakfast. When I asked him what was wrong, he replied that he wasn't happy with his fiancée and was going to call off things with her. I was so excited, but I tried to keep my face from showing it.

The following days of skiing were great. Steve and I would try to sit next to each other on the lift or at dinner so that we could talk. I could tell he was really nervous, although I was still unsure if he was really interested in me. Maybe he thought I was too young for him. I was still in college and in a sorority, and he was working full-time running his personal business, so I was in a different phase of life than he was.

The evening before we were to head back to Orlando, Steve and I decided to build a snowman. Dr. Ross said it couldn't be done with the type of snow that had fallen— it was too dry—so of course we decided to show him! In fact the snow was so dry that it took us two hours just to get the first two balls of the snowman together, but it was a great time to get to know each other better. We both learned a lot and realized we had more in common than anyone else we had ever met. It was a great bonding experience, and we realized we were falling for each other. After two hours, it was time to go to dinner. When my dad saw we hadn't gotten too far on building our snowman, he laughed and popped a road cone on top of the snowman for his head. It was great!

The last night of our vacation, I decided to give Steve my contact information. I handed him a piece of paper with my number, e-mail, and AIM information. In my mind I was hoping he would want to call me for a date or something, but I told him if he ever needed to talk or just wanted to hang out sometime that he should give me a call. The next morning we boarded the plane to head back to Orlando. We flirted with each other the entire plane ride back. It was fun but inside my heart was breaking because the next day I would head back to Jacksonville and didn't know if we would ever see each other again. As we got off the plane in Orlando, we headed down to the luggage claim. Steve and I stayed a little behind my dad and Dr. Ross, and very nonchalantly Steve handed me his business card with all his information. I didn't really know what to think except, *At least I have his number now.* There was no guarantee he would ever call.

Steve's ride was running late and I really wanted to drive him home, but I knew it probably wouldn't be appropriate since his fiancée would be there. It wasn't long before my mom came to pick up Dad and me. She gave me a big hug, and suddenly it was time to say good-bye to Steve.

That night I stayed in Orlando at my parents' house. The next morning I would have to drive back to Jacksonville for classes. I just couldn't help myself that night, so I decided to text Steve and ask if he got home all right. I never received an answer, so I wrote him an e-mail letting him know what a great time I had and how happy I was that I met him. The next morning I got an e-mail back from him, and that's when the communication really started. He told his fiancée that he didn't think their relationship was meant to be and she moved out. For the next couple of days, we would continue to write to each other. Eventually we started to talk on the phone for hours each night. I grew farther and farther apart from my boyfriend at the time and eventually called things off.

One day I invited Steve to come see me in Jacksonville. He was so nervous but actually did come for a visit. We had lunch at Angie's Subs. (He was so nervous he couldn't eat.) In the following weeks, Steve and I continued to talk and learn more about each other. From that weekend on, we haven't spent one weekend apart. It was challenging driving back and forth from Orlando to Jacksonville, but we were both so in love with each other that it didn't matter.

Steve and I loved to go to a restaurant on the beach called Sunny Caribbean. We would sit outside and eat while listening to the ocean. One night after we ate, we decided to take a walk on the beach. After walking for a little bit, we sat on top of a lifeguard tower and listened to the ocean waves. It was dark and cloudy out without a soul around. Steve put his arms around me and held me tight. He looked into my eyes and said, "I had really pictured this different. I wanted to tell you this under the stars on a perfect night, but I love you. I love you so much!"

I was so taken back that I didn't know what to say. After the shock subsided I immediately said, "I love you too!" Right as we said those three words, I looked up in the sky to see thousands of stars shining right above us. One minute it was so cloudy and the next minute the stars were illuminating the sky. It was like a sign that we were really supposed to be together.

It took awhile for my dad to warm up to Steve. We were six years apart in age and Dad really couldn't get past the age difference. Our first Christmas together was wonderful—until the day after Christmas. Steve and I got into a little tiff with my parents and as a result did not talk with them for months. I went through a lot of counseling, and after months of not talking, we were all finally able to come to terms with each other. Steve and Dad had lunch together and talked things through, and the relationship between all of us started over. It would have been so easy for Steve to walk away; instead he stuck by me through everything. He never once said it was too tough.

I graduated from college in May 2007. My entire family drove up to attend the ceremony, and the next day I moved back to Orlando. That night my family took Steve and me out to dinner at the Cheesecake Factory to celebrate and then we went back to the house to open gifts. My parents gave me a book of photographs of New York City. Finally I realized they were giving me not just a book—but a trip to New York. My parents and I would leave the following weekend, which was perfect since Steve was going to be in Texas for a business trip.

As soon as we arrived in New York, Steve's good friend, Phil, who is like a brother to him, and Phil's girlfriend, Kristine, met us at the airport. They had both taken time off work to show us around the big city for the day. And it was a long day! Phil took us everywhere possible and stopped at every stand to get something to eat. The guy has an appetite like I have never seen. They first took us into Brooklyn to get the best pizza ever. Then we headed into the city for some sightseeing. Toward the end of the day, my parents said our last stop would be the Empire State Building. I really wanted to save it for the next day because I was exhausted, but everyone insisted we do it that day. It didn't take too long to get to the top, and once we were up there, the sight was amazing.

I started to walk around the platform at the top of the building to see the city from every angle when my dad came running up to me. "Look there!" he said pointing over the edge. I couldn't see what he was pointing at, but he seemed so excited, so I just kept looking. I felt a tap on my shoulder but didn't turn around because I didn't want to miss whatever my dad was so excited about.

After the second tap, I turned around—and there was Steve. He handed me a rose, and before I could say anything, he got down on one knee right in front of me. I couldn't figure out what he was doing and kept trying to pull him to his feet. Suddenly I spotted a small box in his hand—and I realized what was happening. I was so shocked that I could barely hear the words coming from his mouth as he asked me to marry him. I started crying and replied yes, but it was so soft that no one heard me. Finally someone shouted, "Did she say yes?" This time I said, "Yes!" really loud.

I looked up and there was a crowd around us. They were all taking our pictures; we felt like celebrities. The parents of Steve's best friend were there along with my parents and Phil and Kristine. It was perfect! The celebration moved to Brooklyn where we had a wonderful engagement party at an Italian restaurant.

After dinner Steve told me how he pulled off this surprise. I told him I had gotten a little suspicious about his supposed business trip to Texas because he wasn't giving me much information and hadn't asked me to come along. He knew I was a snooper and would try to find out the truth if he was hiding something, so he got my parents in on the task of trying to throw me off. They kept talking about how hot it would be in Texas and even gave him suggestions of where to go for good Mexican food. Steve even went so far as to leave a day before I did—except he actually flew to New York, not to Texas. He really did a great job of trying to cover his steps.

After we got back from New York, the wedding planning started. I can't believe how much work it is to plan a wedding and especially without a wedding planner.

I already had an idea of the kind of wedding I wanted and started putting together an organized notebook. At first, Steve and I decided on a small wedding in a chapel in downtown Orlando, but as the plans started getting underway, we realized it was going to be bigger than we had originally thought, so we had to move it to a bigger chapel. It seemed as if I had countless appointments with various vendors and had to make many decisions fast. I wanted it to be a day to remember.

Uniting Our Love
December 30, 2007

The day we dream of,
A girl's fantasy;
A perfect walk
Centered on me.
Hours of planning,
Nights of dreams;
Sleepless again,
Forever it seems.
Counting the days,
It's approaching fast;
Together with my honey,
Forever at last.
Dressed in white,
Sheer across my face;
A princess A-lined dress,

Beaded down with lace.
Pearly white strands
Draped around my neck;
Not failing with detail,
Down to every last speck.
Together at the altar
Hand in hand;
Waves of emotion
As here we stand.
A love so strong
Bound with God;
Family and friends
Sharing in our love.
Tears of happiness
Stream down my face;
Together we say, "I do."
With the exchanging of rings.
Married at last,
Headed for our honeymoon;
Leaving for our cruise
And later to kiss beneath the moon.

The evening before our wedding, we had our rehearsal dinner at Dubsdread Country Club in Orlando. It was so great to have our closest friends and family together the night before our big day. The morning of January 5, 2008, I couldn't sleep and woke up especially early. My dad had gone to breakfast with Steve (he was so nervous he didn't eat a bite!) and a couple of the guys to help calm him down. My mom made my favorite breakfast: blueberry waffles. I almost never get so nervous that I can't eat, but this particular morning I just couldn't bring myself to put a bite into my mouth.

Kathy, my mom's good friend, came over early to help my mom with her makeup and dress. My bridesmaids were all at the salon getting their hair done, and Steve went shooting with the guys. So that left me all alone with butterflies in my tummy and hours to spare before having to get ready for my wedding. When I get even a little bit nervous there is only one thing to help calm me down: shopping! So I went to Target and bought a clutch and a new pair of silver shoes for our honeymoon. Those made me feel a lot better. Early in the afternoon I went to get my hair done and meet up with my bridesmaids.

Kathy came to pick us up to take us to the church. We were a little bit late, and I later found out that Steve asked someone to make sure I was still coming. The church was absolutely beautiful! I finished getting ready as many of my close friends and family came in to see me. I kept asking how Steve was doing because I thought he was going to be very nervous. He hates to get in front of a large group of people, and he was about to stand in front of almost 200 guests. Surprisingly, I was told that he wasn't nervous at all and couldn't wait to get the wedding started.

The ceremony started at 5:00 p.m. Right before we were about to begin it started to sprinkle outside. I was so happy because I heard it was good luck if it rains on your wedding day. We all lined up as the seating of the family took place. I could see the groomsmen standing at the front of the church and then I saw Steve. I was finally marrying the man of my dreams.

The wedding party started to walk the aisle. When it came time for my dad to walk me to the altar, he started to tear up. He told me he thought I was doing the right thing by marrying Steve and that I looked beautiful. It was great to have my dad by my side on one of the most important days of my life. As we approached the altar, the pastor started to speak. When he asked who gives this lady away, my dad replied, "Her mother and I do." Steve was supposed to come and take my hand from my dad, but he forgot and my dad had to motion for him. It was quite humorous.

Immediately following the wedding, we took more pictures and headed off to our reception at the Orlando Country Club. Steve and I had prepared a surprise choreographed dance for our first dance together. We had practiced for months and finally learned how to do the fox trot. When it came time for our first dance, Steve was so nervous he could barely talk to me. We danced to "New York, New York" by Frank Sinatra. The guests were hooting and hollering and really enjoyed our performance.

Later we enjoyed speeches by my sister, Steve's best man, and my dad. It was definitely a tear-jerker! The reception lasted well into the night. In fact, the DJ had to coax people off the dance floor because it was getting so late. He motioned all our guests outside the country club to get ready to send us off with sparklers and bubbles. While they did that, Steve and I had one last slow, romantic dance together with no one around.

Next thing I knew we were running out of the country club and into a limo. (We had to actually turn around and go back to the country club after we took off because Steve forgot his wallet and keys!) January 5, 2008, we started our life together as Mr. and Mrs. Steven Rowell.

The next day we took off to Miami to catch a cruise to the southern Caribbean. We boarded the ship and headed for our room, which was decorated with colorful balloons, banners, and cake. My parents surprised us with a nice bottle of wine and chocolate-covered strawberries. The cruise was so much fun, and we were able to visit many unique places. We also had a great view from our balcony so at night we would have a glass of wine and sit outside. We spent a week on the cruise, and when we got back we moved all my belongings into Steve's house (now our house) and began our life journey together.

Chapter 7

A Voice

IT WAS CERTAINLY A whirlwind year. In a span of about eight months, I graduated, moved back to Orlando, got engaged, planned my wedding, got married, started my master's program, and started a new job. Guess what the job was? Working in a psychiatric facility as a mental health technician. I worked in inpatient units with some of the worst cases, and I enjoyed every minute of it. Not only was I able to learn many new and exciting things working within the mental health field, but I was also able to help the population I longed to help based on everything I had gone through myself. At times the days drained me, but I reminded myself that God had placed me there for a reason and every day made a difference when I was able to help others.

I worked there for more than a year and created a group therapy program for the patients. I was even able to facilitate some of the groups. This experience reaffirmed my desire to work with the mental health population.

After a year I decided it would be more beneficial to work for the same organization but in the fund-raising department, which allowed me to help raise money and awareness for the behavioral health center. As I write this book, I am working full-time, just graduated with my master's degree in mental health counseling, and now am finishing my practicum working with sexual abuse victims. And there's another huge change about to happen in my life: Steve and I are expecting our first baby boy, Preston Marshall Rowell. We are thrilled to become new parents. I just hope I will be able to help my child through every one of life's trials as others have helped me in the past.

I would not have been able to do any of this with such a strong passion unless I had traveled the road I did. Every experience I had was a divine intervention from God to guide me down a path to help others. I am so thankful I had the love and support of my family and friends to get me through my troubled years. I can only pray that God will continue to use me for His kingdom to help others.

As I started my journey, I had not yet accepted Christ as my Lord and Savior. In fact, I was involved in the complete opposite of what He wanted for me. I learned to cut to externalize my internal pain. I have been down a road of pure evil and destruction, but through the grace of our Lord and Savior I was saved and am now His daughter. I have surrendered my life to Christ, knowing He allowed me to continue down a crooked path for a purpose. God judged it better to bring good out of evil than to not let evil happen. "I consider that our present sufferings are not worth comparing with the glory that will be revealed in us" (Rom. 8:18). A true benefit to having suffered is being able to help others going through something similar.

Every life has meaning and a purpose. Each one of us is unique and has his or her own set of strengths that can be used for the greater good of society. I believe everything happens for a reason. If we are going through hard times, it will make us stronger, and we will learn how to handle future situations. When bad things happen, although it may be unpleasant and hurtful, God will not give us more than we can handle. If we have faith and trust, we can get through anything.

You may be experiencing something similar to what I have gone through. Perhaps you feel completely hope-less. I am here to tell you that where there is pain, there is hope! We may not always know or understand what or why we are going through tough times, but reaching for help and support can help get you through your time of need.

For years I have done a tremendous amount of soul-searching and self-discovery. I believe I was put on this earth to serve Christ and others through Him. I believe His purpose for my life was predetermined to prepare me to help those who do not have a voice. He has allowed me to endure circumstances involving mental health issues so that I would gain experience and understanding for my journey to becoming a mental health professional. My life is a gift, and I have been given an open book to write from beginning to end. Life is like drawing without an eraser, and each stage brings new and exciting challenges with opportunities for positive change.

Many of my personality traits came from my family. My mother has always been a hardworking woman and has climbed her way up the executive ladder. She has instilled in me the drive to always strive for excellence, even in the worst circumstances. My father has always taught persistence as a key skill to have throughout life. I am very persistent and love a challenge. I have formed my identity from the assets my parents have instilled in me. I know there is no one just like me, and therefore I must strive to do the best I can to touch others' lives in a positive manner.

I want to make a difference as a mental health counselor. I plan to do this by reducing stigma, raising awareness and funds for the mental health field, creating a better environment within the inpatient setting, and inspiring the lives of those seeking counseling. I plan to become a licensed mental health counselor working within the clinical field. I would also like to eventually start a mental health foundation to raise money for individuals who are unable to afford the costs of counseling or other mental health services. I believe I am on the right track.

I have gained various strengths and insights based on the many challenges I have experienced thus far. Once a young girl who was naïve and dependent, I have grown into a woman with confidence and passion for life. I have learned how it feels to experience pain and to give pain, how to love others unconditionally and to maintain a desire to enrich the lives of those I encounter. I know I will make a wonderful wife, mother, sister, granddaughter, and counselor and will give my all until the day I am no longer called to.

A Note to Those Hurting

I KNOW YOU'RE SEARCHING FOR something more in this world. I know it hurts emotionally and physically. I know you feel alone and think no one understands what you are going through. I know...I was there!

I don't want my story to sound as if I went through so much horror and then all of a sudden I was cured, because that would be inaccurate. I have to honestly tell you that although I have come a long way from where I started, I still struggle mildly today. I am no longer on medication for depression; however, I occasionally struggle with panic attacks when I become overwhelmed or stressed. I always have an anti-anxiety medication on hand just in case I ever need it, and occasionally I do.

I also struggle with my appearance from time to time. I am now at a healthy weight but often have distorted thoughts of my body image. I just keep reminding myself that I am beautiful and don't need to go to extremes to be thin. I have to be careful when I do go on diets because my old habits quickly come rushing back. There are times when I look in the mirror and think I am extremely overweight, but instead of being unhealthy I tell my husband my thoughts so that I can receive his support.

As far as cutting, I have done a complete turnaround. The scars I have are barely visible. I think I am really the only one who can see them because I am the one who made them. Although I no longer cut, there are times when life can get me very down, and immediately my thoughts turn to what I knew. I know this is something I will continue to battle in my thoughts, but I also know I have overcome the physical aspect and only faint scars remain.

Other past experiences have left me. I am no longer into alcohol, drugs, or witchcraft. I try to keep myself from falling back into my old ways by telling my story. It helps to reinforce how far I have come by saying it aloud. My past will always be something I cannot change, but my future holds promising experiences to help others.

I recently accepted a job position, in Orlando, where I will have the opportunity to live out my dream of counseling children and adolescents through the use of play therapy. I know I will make it my mission to be the voice for those who do not feel they have a voice.

I encourage everyone to speak with a counselor at some point in their life. And let me start with you. Please know there is help and there is hope. Hold on to the little bit of wonder inside you telling you that there is something better out there, and then search for it. If you are experiencing the same things I did, I advise you to fight against the hopeless feelings that threaten to overwhelm you. Try to find one positive glimpse of hope to hold on to. "And hope maketh not ashamed" (Rom. 5:5a, KJV).

Looking back I believe if I would have disclosed the many experiences I had, I would have been diagnosed with Post-Traumatic Stress Disorder (PTSD). This is in an important concept to understand because you may know someone who has or you may have PTSD without knowing it, and it is extremely vital to seek professional help. PTSD occurs when someone has experienced a traumatic event involving actual or threatened death or injury, or a threat to one's integrity followed by intense fear or helplessness, such as being raped. This is according to DSM IV, the diagnostic manual for mental disorders. There are many characteristics involved with PTSD. Some of the ones I experienced were distressing memories of my rape experience, flashbacks, and nightmares.

If you have been exposed to a traumatic event and think you may be experiencing some of the symptoms of PTSD, I encourage you to seek professional help. I did not disclose being raped until seven years after it had happened. If I would have sought help earlier, I could have prevented the longevity of the symptoms I was experiencing.

Surround yourself with others who are the opposite of how you are feeling. Don't let yourself be alone. Reach for something more and explore what Christ has in store for you. Believe me, it's something big!

A Note to Parents and Loved Ones of Those Hurting

THERE ARE CERTAIN INDICATORS that you can look for if you suspect your teen is struggling.

There has to be a balance between tough love and comforting. We all make mistakes, but I would like to share with you a few things my parents did right when going through this journey with me.

I firmly believe it is important to shut out all negative outside influences. What I mean by this is to limit the forces that go against your family values. My parents did well by limiting my contact with my negative peer group. Those friends taught me a lot of what I knew. I was getting mixed messages from what my friends believed and what my parents had brought me up to believe. That's why it is important to watch and listen.

Watch out for changes in behavior and attitude in your teen. You can see this in many different ways. You may start to see a change in the friends whom your teen chooses. She may stop hanging out with her regular group of friends and choose another group such as friends who are older than she is. You may see a negative shift in her mood during this time. Her mood may go from pleasant to depressed or defiant. If a difference or fluctuation in mood is evident, it is important for you to assess for suicidal ideations and self-injurious behaviors.

Listen for statements such as, "I hate my life and don't want to live anymore." If you hear this, take it seriously and make it a priority to have a conversation with your teen.

Watch cough, cold, and prescription medications in your home. Self-injurious behaviors may include self-medicating through medications already in your house. Also watch the way your teen dresses. Adolescents who cut themselves tend to wear long-sleeved shirts and dress in colors that reflect their mood, such as black for depression.

If you suspect cutting, nonchalantly check your teen's arms, legs, thighs, stomach, wrists, and ankles. These are just a few common places found in those who cut. Adolescents who cut themselves will most likely have scars from picking off the scabs. Cutting usually occurs when one is feeling so low that she uses cutting as a means to get her anger to surface. It becomes a release for the pain she is feeling. If you suspect your teen is engaging in self-injurious behaviors, do not panic, at least not in front of her. Instead, take a calm approach by explaining that you understand she is hurting and in pain. Explain that you can understand how harming herself is a release of that pain, but that you are concerned about her and would like her to pursue, with your help, professional mental health services.

If you are close to someone who cuts, I encourage you not to display disappointment or feelings of disgust. Instead love her where she is and show her you don't look down on her or think she is weird because she has chosen to express herself through cutting. The last thing you want to do is make her think she is not normal. I am not saying you have to condone the action, but she will most likely continue to cut whether you like it or not.

My mom showed me she loved me unconditionally when she personally rubbed oil on my scars. She stayed by my side even when it looked as if there was truly no hope left. I would have to compare her actions to the story in the Bible when Jesus showed the full extent of His love by washing His disciples' feet before His final hour (see John 13:2-4). Jesus, the Son of God, should have had His feet washed by His disciples. Instead He showed that love is laying down one's life. Loving completely means to love to the end of one's life. As a teenager, I should have been the one showing respect to my mother. Instead my mother showed me that despite her disapproval of my choice to harm myself, she was still able to love me through it all. A family photo hangs in my parent's house, and if you look closely you are able to see the outline of the word *Vampire* that I had carved in my arm. Yet she took care of me so that the physical scars would become less visible. To this day it is hard to tell that I was ever a cutter.

As you watch for changes in mood, remember that adolescents strive for independence and will push you away every chance they get. They may even say hurtful statements directed toward you such as, "I hate you." It is important for parents and/or caregivers to realize these statements are usually made to be interpreted in the opposite of their meaning. Adolescents may push you away, but inside they are crying for your support and help. Do not leave your teen during this emotional time. Instead let her know you are with her physically and emotionally and will never give up on her.

Another area to "listen and watch" are phone calls, texting, and Internet usage. Although my parents didn't have to worry too much about my Internet use because it wasn't as popular as it is today, I strongly suggest parents monitor their children's social networks on the Web. It never feels good to have "big brother" constantly watching over you, but when you are in this type of situation, I believe it is best to know who your child is conversing with on a daily basis.

This also applies to searching your teen's room. Based on experience, I would highly suggest if you are going to search through her room that you not make it known to her. The reasons for this are simple. The less she knows that you know about her life, the easier it will be to find information. For instance, if I knew my parents were regularly searching my room, I would have distrusted them even more than I already did and would have come up with new and innovative ways to hide things from them.

Pay attention to the times your child does begin to talk to you. When I got my driver's permit, my mother drove with me wherever I went and used that opportunity to talk with me—and to listen to what I was saying.

Another important note is to pick and choose your battles. It was important for my parents to limit my contact with outside negative influences; however, fighting about the clothes I wore was not a battle my parents decided to pick. I usually wore all black every day. By my parents choosing to allow me to continue this trend, they were giving me the opportunity to have my own identity. This gave me an outlet to express myself when other outlets were taken away. It also gave me a sense of control over who I was.

Finally, as parents remember that you have the spiritual authority over your children. Pray for them and over them for their guidance and protection. My mother would sneak into my room at night while I was sleeping and place her hand on my feet and pray over me. I can't stress how important this is. If you do nothing else, pray. Your child doesn't even have to know you are praying for or over her. In fact, I probably wouldn't do it at a time she is aware because it may drive her even farther away.

Don't underestimate the power of the prayers of a parent. Jesus said, "Behold, I give you the authority to trample on serpents and scorpions, and over all the power of the enemy, and nothing shall by any means hurt you" (Luke 10:19 NKJV). As much as your child may wish for you not to help her, there is something to be said for the parent who exerts control over a difficult situation involving his or her child. Every parent has the right to know who his or her child is hanging out with, what type of music and television shows she is listening to/watching, and where she is at all times. It becomes problematic when parents know these facts about their child yet choose to live in denial and not take action.

Parents, you do have legal rights over your children who are under eighteen years of age. When all else fails and you are in a crisis, there are two main legal options you should be aware of.

A Baker Act in the state of Florida should be initiated when your teen is displaying suicidal and/or homicidal ideations. If you believe your teen is in serious danger of harming herself or other people and you feel action should be initiated immediately, you can initiate the Baker Act. You can do this by calling law enforcement and explaining the suicidal and/or homicidal ideations your teen is displaying. Law enforcement will pick up your teen and bring her to the nearest Baker Act receiving facility where she can be held for psychological evaluation for up to seventy-two hours. Advantages of the Baker Act are immediate safety, psychological assessment, medical evaluation, and possible entry to group or individual therapy.

The next option available to you is the Marchman Act. The Marchman Act is initiated for individuals in need of treatment for substance abuse. By law a minor is able to seek treatment for substance abuse without the permission of a parent or caregiver. However, an involuntary admission for treatment through the Marchman Act can be initiated when an individual is impaired by a substance and has lost control or is threatening to inflict harm on herself or others. The Marchman Act is used for those suffering from substance abuse.

To initiate the Marchman Act, you should file a Marchman Act petition with the court, and within ten days a hearing will be set. A judge will decide if the person in question will need to be placed involuntarily in a substance-abuse treatment facility. If a judge decides it is best for involuntary admission to a treatment facility, a law officer, in regular street clothes, will be sent to detain the individual for treatment. A person may be held for assessment and observation in a substance-abuse treatment facility for up to five days.

The Baker Act and the Marchman Act are great resources for you to utilize in crisis with your troubled teen. Please research the above options to make the best informed decision.

Friend to Friend

I F YOU ARE A friend of someone going through a difficult time, signs may be more evident for you. Your friends will most likely disclose their feelings and thoughts more readily to you than they would to their parents. They may show you their scars from injuring themselves or tell you they are feeling depressed.

Take these signs seriously, and seek help from a trusted adult. If you can, do not break your friends' trust by going behind their backs, but instead explain to your friends that you care about them and want to be with them every step of the way. If they know they will have a friend with them through this difficult time, they will be more prone to receiving help.

Parent to Parent

I ASKED MY MOTHER TO write something that would help other parents who are dealing with the same issues that she and my dad dealt with.

Having read Shannon's story, you might find it helpful to hear about my journey as a parent going through this very difficult time with a child I loved dearly but who had become a stranger to me. I hope that what I learned in trying to help Shannon will be beneficial to you. What I will share with you is, of course, just a reflection of my own experience, and every situation is different.

If you face a similar ordeal with your child, the first thing I would say to you is never give up hope. During these trying times your child needs you more than ever. Hope is the beacon of light in the midst of these darkest of times. This is what I have learned as a parent in trying to help Shannon.

As Shannon described, she was a wonderfully happy, easy-going child. My husband and I raised Shannon and her sister with the

Christian values and beliefs that we both share. They were involved in Sunday school, church, and youth group, and they both went to Christian schools. As I learned, this is not an insurance policy that will keep your child from straying off the right path. Yet although Shannon strayed from these core beliefs, I believe that the Christian foundation she had growing up eventually helped her turn her life around. The Bible speaks about this in Proverbs 22:6: "Train a child in the way he should go, and when he is old he will not turn from it."

The first sign of trouble was when Shannon started attending a youth group where she met some peers who were involved with the occult. Of course, I didn't know that until much later. After meeting these kids, she began to dress in all black and lost a lot of weight, and her personality really began to change. This evolved over the course of the year into depression, cutting, half-hearted suicide attempts, and complete withdrawal from the family. Any interactions we did have resulted in Shannon yelling, screaming, and name-calling. It was the lowest point of my life for sure.

Through this time I was in constant prayer asking God to break the chains of darkness that were imprisoning my daughter. This wasn't something I could have talked about to anyone except my husband and one or two friends, so it was a very lonely time. However, feeling so alone made me reach out to God in a way that I had never done before. I had always been a Christian, but I'd never been tested to the point that I had to totally trust Him. Now I needed to trust Him with my daughter's life.

During this time of prayer, God revealed to me several actions that my husband and I needed to take. Thus began the tough but unrelenting love approach with Shannon. The first thing God told me to do was to find all her CDs and throw them out. I decided to listen to a few before I did that and was appalled at what I heard. Songs about killing others and yourself, profane and disgusting lyrics about women, sex, etc. I threw them all out and took away the CD player and radio. It was like God telling me to purge our house of the evil influences Shannon had brought into the home. Probably like most parents, I was unaware of what my children were listening to and watching on television.

Second, He told me to go through Shannon's room and read everything I could find and look for objects that represented evil. I found pentagrams, witchcraft books, and poems that

Shannon had written about vampires, cutting, and death. I was shaken to the core after finding all of this, but it made me understand how deep into the darkness Shannon really was.

When you find your child in these circumstances, you have a choice to make. I hear the debate on talk shows all the time about whether you should respect your child's privacy and therefore not snoop around in his or her room. My opinion is that when you trust your child and things are going well, it is good to respect their privacy, but when you have suspicions or red flags about what is going on in your child's life, I strongly believe that you must use every possible way to find out the truth. Your child's life may depend on it; Shannon's did!

Also, when facing the truth about what your child is into, you need to decide if you are going to be the parent who loves her child enough to exhibit tough, caring love or you are going to try to be your child's friend. My experience with Shannon reinforced to me that she needed parents who would be firm and unwavering in our efforts to bring her back around. Believe me, this wasn't easy, but with God's help we were able to do it. I've talked to so many parents in this situation, and more often than not I've seen that they were not able to step up and take the approach of tough, caring love. The parents who have sought my advice over the years and have been able to assume this approach have been much more successful in helping their child get through this very difficult time. Other parents either were so angry at their child that they couldn't inject the "love" into "tough love," or they just tried to be their child's friend through it all. As you heard from Shannon's perspective, the fact that we were able to hold true to a firm but loving approach helped her end up where she is today.

If you have a spouse, make sure you talk about your roles in dealing with your child. There needs to be a "good cop, bad cop" approach. In our relationship, my husband was the firm hand, and although I was also firm, I tried to engage with Shannon on different levels. She was very uncommunicative during this time, so I would look for ways to get her to talk. It turned out that driving in the car was the only time she would open up, so we would drive around endlessly on some days and nights just so that I could get a sense of what she was thinking. Find those opportunities with your child. It may mean lying on the floor of their room talking to them, driving, or even engaging in physical sports. Just keep trying to find an environment that is non-threatening and conducive to allowing you to get an idea of where your child is.

Although the times I had with Shannon in the car were mostly calm and reasonable, there were times when she would have huge emotional outbursts and tell me she hated me. Those were devastating words to me, but I refused to give up on her. I would grab her shoulders and look at her and say, "I know this isn't my child talking. I love you and I'll never give up hope for you—never!" Even though she would turn away from me and leave after these encounters, today Shannon says that my words and emotion still got through to her.

Shannon was fourteen years old at the time and was living in our house, so we had more control over her environment than someone whose child lives outside the house, but the same principles in dealing with a child in this situation could apply. An absolute key to Shannon's turnaround was disconnecting her from her peers who were so deeply involved in all the bad things that she needed to break free from. We took her out of school, and my husband homeschooled her. We put her on "house arrest" for a time. We took away her cell phone, and I even went to a spy store and picked up a device that monitored incoming as well as outgoing calls. We took her TV out of her room and took the door off her bedroom hinges so that we could observe her.

As you can imagine, she rebelled vehemently against all this, but we stuck to our guns. She was only allowed to go out of the house with us. We allowed her to go to our church's youth group, but we sat out front on the steps to make sure she didn't run away.

During this time, Shannon was suffering from severe depression, and along with cutting she made a half-hearted attempt at suicide by ingesting ibuprofen. She was hospitalized in a behavioral health center. While in the hospital, she met other teens who shared some of her issues, and they shared things they were doing, which gave Shannon more ideas, such as cutting. I first learned of this one day when I walked in on her while she was in the bathtub. I saw the scabs on her arm that outlined the word *vampire*. I thought I was going to faint on the spot as it was so incredibly distressing to me. What could be worse than a Christian family having a young daughter carve on her arm something that related to the occult?

I was overwhelmed with grief, but the grief made me pray and seek God even more.

Shannon did continue her cutting behavior for quite some time, and I came to understand that cutting wasn't really a suicide attempt but a way of releasing emotional pain. Cutting was her way of showing us the deep turmoil that was going on inside her. Cutting isn't talked about very much, but I believe it is pretty common and one of the reasons Shannon wrote this book. This subject is still associated with a terrible stigma, so there is not much written about it. I couldn't find any books on the subject when I was researching how to help Shannon. If your child is engaging in this type of behavior, my advice is not to freak out but instead just get them the help that they need.

At this time we were meeting with various counselors who were not much help. No one could get to the root of her depression and Goth-type behavior. Of course, Marshall and I had no idea at this time that she had gotten so deeply into witchcraft, and I didn't find out until two years ago that Shannon had been raped.

We took Shannon home and got back into the "house-arrest" mode. Because Shannon was so depressed, I slept with her every night to make sure she didn't harm herself. Even though I'd get mad at her for her behavior and attitude,

I just kept telling her, "I'm not going to give up on you." I prayed for her every waking moment that I could and cried out to God to please heal Shannon and reunite us as a family.

Although I wanted with all my heart to believe this would happen, I was beginning to wrestle with the fact that there was a possibility we might lose Shannon. I spent many days and nights sitting in my closet crying and praying. (Our house was so chaotic that it was the only place I could find some solitude.)

Even though my husband and I were coping with this situation very differently, we did work hard to support each other during this time. His quiet hugs meant so much to me. If you are a couple going through this, know that it will test your marriage to the breaking point if you don't figure out a joint game plan on how to handle your child and how to support each other. Satan would like nothing better than to break up your marriage during this time of attack on your family.

Seeking professional help is critical when your child is withdrawn, depressed, or cutting. Shannon saw a psychiatrist regularly and was on high doses of antidepressants. We were referred to several counselors, but most of them had a secular view, which was, "It's a stage. She will grow out of it. Give her some room and don't be too strict." I knew through my prayer time and verses that God gave me such as Proverbs 3:5-7 that this counsel was the opposite of what God was leading us to do, so we didn't continue counseling as a family.

Having said this, I know counselors can be very helpful in situations with rebellious and depressed teenagers. Just make sure that you find someone who shares your perspective about how to help your child. No one knows your child better than you do. You have to assume the advocacy role for your child in these types of circumstance. If you are a Christian, I would really suggest seeking out a Christian counselor who is experienced but young enough to relate to your child. Shannon had a great Christian counselor who ended up helping her and who communicated well with us. We will be eternally grateful for her help. It was this counselor who went with Shannon, my husband, and me to see a pastor at our church who specialized in helping troubled kids, especially those who had been involved in cult activities. He talked straight to Shannon and told her and us that the chance of coming out of this dark side was about 10 percent in his experience—unless Shannon was willing to acknowledge to

God all she had been involved in and ask for forgiveness.

After I heard this, I remember having an out-of-body experience during the rest of our meeting because the odds he was giving us were so low. Shannon did pray with him, but I think it was more out of fear than anything else. When we got home I remember asking her if I could pray with her asking God to intervene in her life and she said yes. Things began to get a little better after that, but she was still wearing black all the time and was depressed—but not as angry and rebellious as before.

A few months later we were in an evening service at our church. Shannon didn't want to sit next to us, so she sat at the end of a pew with a girl she had met. In all honesty, I was surprised this girl had reached out to her because Shannon was pretty scary looking in all her Goth dress and accessories. I remain thankful to her for loving Shannon when it wasn't easy to love Shannon.

At the end of the service, the pastor had us pray, and he offered an invitation for people to come up front and give their lives to Christ, which supposedly Shannon had done in third grade. When we opened our eyes after the prayer, I looked over at Shannon and she was gone! I started to cry because I thought she had run away as she had done before when we were in church. I turned to my husband and told him we needed to find her. As we were getting up, someone came up to us and asked if we were looking for Shannon and said she had come forward at the pastor's invitation to accept Christ as her Lord and Savior. I began to sob uncontrollably. I was so thankful to God for this miracle. This was the turning point and the start of her healing process.

As the months progressed, Shannon's attitude began to change, her depression started lifting, and we began to have talks about how she could regain our trust. She had hurt our family deeply, including her younger sister, and we told her she would have to prove to us over time that we could trust her. Until then there would continue to be many restrictions on whom she could see and talk to, and she wasn't allowed to go anywhere by herself, except to the house of one Christian friend.

A few months later she handed me all her black clothes and said she didn't need them anymore. That was one happy day! Shannon then began attending a Christian high school and became a cheerleader, which helped her become once again the child we knew. It was about this time that she felt God's strong calling to pursue a degree in mental health counseling. She never wavered from this, and now has achieved that goal and will be helping others who are going through the things she experienced. I know she will be a great counselor because of her experience, and she will be able to offer hope to others.

Here are some of the lessons I learned as a parent through Shannon's journey:

- Never give up hope!

- Advocate for your child; you know them best.

- Trust God and engage in intercessory prayer for your child. If your child is living in your house, you still have spiritual authority over them.

- Be the parent they need, not the friend they want.

- Control the environment and limit external influences.

- Seek out young, experienced Christian counselors who can relate to your child.

- Forgive yourself for the mistakes you make.

- If you are married, work out the game plan with your spouse and support each other through this.

- Don't neglect other members of the family. Unfortunately our younger daughter felt neglected during this time because we were so wrapped up in trying to save Shannon's life. She has struggled with some of the memories of that time and only recently has begun her healing process. In hindsight we really should have been more available and supportive to her during this time as well. We didn't realize that she was feeling so vulnerable at that time, but this reinforces the fact that situations like this impact the entire family in different ways.

- Don't let your anger toward your child cause you to become bitter and unapproachable. Remember your child needs you more than ever during this time. If you become angry and bitter, the chances of your child turning his or her life around become less. You are the lifeline, whether your child deserves it or not.

I understand the pain and emotional roller coaster that a prodigal child brings. Having gone through this, I truly know what it means to have your heart broken. However, don't give up hope, no matter what. As you have read in Shannon's story, it is possible through tough, caring love and prayer to break the chains that hold your child from the life God intended them to have. Remember, nothing is impossible with God. I look at Shannon now and marvel at how God took a very dark time in her life and turned it into a beacon of light for others. I am immensely proud of her for having the courage to write this book. She is an inspiration to me!

—Sherrie Sitarik

Showing Your Support: Top 10 Things to Remember

1. Listen: Be an active listener; be genuine and supportive in your statements.

2. Watch: Keep an eye on behavior and attitude changes.

3. Be supportive: Show empathy and understanding when your teen talks to you.

4. Do not judge: Try not to use blaming statements such as "You ___." Instead, use statements such as, "I feel ___."

5. Pray: You have spiritual authority over your teen. Pray for her and for your guidance.

6. Seek professional help: Know your options when in a crisis and engage your teen in the decision-making process when possible.

7. Do not be afraid to take action: You have authority over your teen. Try to be a parent more than a friend to her.

8. Set boundaries: Teens need structure as well as independence. Set rules and consequences in the home.

9. Choose your battles: Choose what is important to you. Think before you act. A good question to remember is, "Will this hurt my teen or my family in any way?"

10. Do not give up: This is the most important. Never give up on your teen. Show her you are with her for the entire journey.

Don't give up! This is the single most important advice I can give to you. My mother never gave up on me, and to this day I appreciate it more than any other thing she has done for me. Your loved one who is hurting may push you away and say some of the most hurtful words to you that you could imagine, but stay by her side. Show her you love her and will never leave her during this tough time. Don't push things on her that she does not want to hear. Instead give it up to God and trust He will take care of each worry you have today. Be her cheerleader. You won't regret it in the end.

Resources

National

National Suicide hotline: 1-800-Suicide (784-2433)

Parent hotline: 1-800-840-6537

National Rape Crisis hotline: 1-800-656-4673

National Drug Information Treatment and Referral hotline: 1-800-662-Help (4357)

Florida

Orlando Crisis/Suicide hotline: (407) 425-2624

Central Florida Center for Drug-Free Living: (407) 245-0014

Lakeside Alternatives: (407) 875-3700

The Healing Tree Sexual Trauma Recovery Center: (407) 317-7430

House of Hope: (407) 843-8686

IF YOU'RE A FAN OF THIS BOOK, PLEASE TELL OTHERS...

- Write about *Chains Be Broken* on your blog, Twitter, MySpace, and Facebook page.

- Suggest *Chains Be Broken* to friends.

- When you're in a bookstore, ask them if they carry the book. The book is available through all major distributors, so any bookstore that does not have *Chains Be Broken* in stock can easily order it.

- Write a positive review of *Chains Be Broken* on www.amazon.com.

- Send my publisher, HigherLife Publishing, suggestions on Web sites, conferences, and events you know of where this book could be offered. Their contact information is listed on the next page.

- Purchase additional copies to give away as gifts. My contact information is listed on the the next page.

CONNECT WITH ME...

To learn more about *Chains Be Broken,* please visit my Web site at **www.chainsbebroken.com** or e-mail me at **ChainsBeBroken@gmx.com**.

You may also contact my Publisher:

HigherLife Development Services
400 Fontana Circle
Building 1 – Suite 105
Oviedo, Florida 32765
Phone: (407) 563-4806
E-mail: media@ahigherlife.com

Help Me Benefit Others...

Because my life has been powerfully and positively impacted through the sincere and trained services of gifted counselors, I want to "give back" by donating to a mental health charity a portion of the proceeds from every book sold. I just wanted you to know that.

Shannon